PUCKER UP!

The Subversive Woman's Guide to Aging With Wit, Wine, Drama, Humor, Perspective, and the Occasional Good Cry

by
Ruth Pennebaker
and
Marian Henley

Female friendship grows more valuable with each passing year. This is for our many women friends who have enriched our lives, saved our lives, and made us laugh till we were candidates for adult diapers.

– R.P. and M.H.

Praise for *PUCKER UP!*

"*Pucker Up!* explores the joys and angst of growing old with insight, heart and soul – and it's hysterically funny. I love this book."

— **Laura Carstensen, Ph.D.,**
Director, Stanford University Center on Longevity, and author of *A Long Bright Future: Happiness, Health, and Financial Security in an Age of Increased Longevity*

"*Pucker Up!* – Ruth Pennebaker's and Marian Henley's funny, wise, smart-alecky, and thoughtful book — is a pick-me-up for women who aren't thrilled about aging. Reading it is just like a raucous visit from your best girlfriends."

— **Margo Howard,**
author of *Eat, Drink & Remarry; Confessions of a Serial Wife*

"Ruth Pennebaker and Marian Henley dispense their wisdom with a delightful dose of hilarity and irreverence in *Pucker Up!* This is strong medicine for what ails us, but medicine never tasted so good. If you're a woman over 50, you need this book. Come to think of it, if you're over 30 you need this book."

—**Lee Robinson,**
author of *Lawyer for the Dog* and *Hearsay*

"I've grown up and old(ish) alongside Ruth and Marian, enjoying their very distinctive perspectives on the stages of our lives over the years. Now this funny, mouthy, and wise book has me almost ready let go of the (ish) and face my age with, if not joy, at least appreciation for what it took for all of us to get here, and everything we've gained along the way. Also comfortable shoes."

— **Sophia Dembling,**
author of *The Introvert's Way: Living a Quiet Life in a Noisy World*

INTRODUCTION

You know how it goes when you're officially No Longer Young.

Some days are great. Spirits are good, body's cooperating, no major emotional or physical breakdowns going on. You don't feel like you're any particular age, so you revert to your default era. Forty-ish, say. Mature, yet frisky.

Other days, forget it. Your joints scream, you crack a molar on a cakeball, you look in a mirror and your mother stares back (either your mother or a shar-pei). All of a sudden, you do feel a particular age and it's astronomical. Mature, yet broken down. You'll need a spatula to get yourself back together.

Being in your 50s, 60s and 70s is like that. At its best, it's a slower, calmer time, when you feel as if a great storm has passed. You have more time for friends, family, pleasure, and work you enjoy. You feel as if you finally understand yourself and your life better.

At its most difficult, friends sicken and die. Your own small illnesses linger a little longer. You forget a name or a face. The outside world is fast and frenzied, but you're a little slower. Or maybe you just don't care about it as much as you used to.

Oh, but what the hell. Life is fleeting and we wanted to write a book with some ideas about trying to age as well as we can – with humor, playfulness, whimsy, subversiveness, and as many insights as we can accrue. Bring on the wine and the wisecracks, howl with grief, love and get laid as much as you can, try to comprehend this whole damned universe and the lives we've been given, laugh, seek to make the world just a little better.

We're calling it *Pucker Up!* since the term sounds too funny not to use, it precedes kissing, it's a very apt description of our skin tone, and because, sometimes, you just have to pucker up and kiss the frog if you want to get anywhere.

Anyway, maybe the whole basis of ideas for aging well is simply living as well as you can for as long as you can. We have wrinkles, we have perspective, we're wiser than we used to be. Why not try to fashion lives that are as rich and meaningful and fun for as long as we can pull it off? Here goes.

– Ruth Pennebaker and Marian Henley

Chapters

One: Let's Get Real

Two: You're Entitled to an ATTITUDE

Three: Stay Flexible About the Whole Damned Thing

Four: Mingle

Five: Dress and Undress

Six: Grab a Quick Fix if Necessary

Seven: Be Prepared

Eight: Be Someone Better

One : Let's Get Real

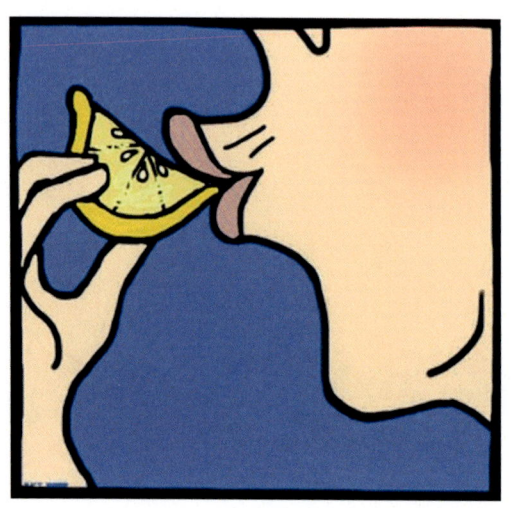

 number 1

Accept the fact you're getting older. Accept it, deal with it, live as fully and well as you can – and stop wasting time and energy denying it.

Remember the American transcendentalist Margaret Fuller? Probably not – but she was given to exclaiming, "I accept the universe!"

"Gad! She'd better," the British writer Thomas Carlisle reportedly said.

The same general principle applies with aging. Why waste your time denying the undeniable? Gad! You've got better things to do.

 number 2

**OK, OK, so it's not that easy to accept aging.
Be patient. Acceptance sinks in like a leaky faucet
– day after day, drip after drip.**

Remember how we pursued feminist "consciousness-raising" in the 1970s? It took awhile, right?

Accepting your age can be just as tough as raising your consciousness.

In fact, you should probably forget the whole leaky faucet comparison. Instead, imagine coming to terms with your age as a journey and not giving a shit as your destination.

 **number 3**

Don't lie about your age to yourself or anybody else. That kind of shady dishonesty will give you wrinkles, backaches, migraines, free-floating anxiety, and a rotten disposition. It may also contribute to global warming. So, tell the truth or take the Fifth Amendment.

Sure, you don't have to blurt out your age if you don't want to. But don't lie about it, either. (A simple, "It's none of your fucking business" should make your stance clear.)

The trouble is, lying about your age robs you of every single marker in your life. Markers like where you were when you learned Kennedy had been assassinated, when you first heard the Beatles, when you listened to the Watergate hearings. Remember images of Sputnik on a small-screen, green-hued TV? Tail fins on 1950s cars, Tic-Tac-Dough, payola, saddle shoes, and summers before air-conditioning? When marijuana was called pot, girls were counseled to find careers "to fall back on," restrooms and water fountains were segregated, and gays were called "queers" – when they were talked about at all.

Those weren't the good old days and life wasn't better then. It was worse, harder, less fair in so many ways.

But those were the times we all lived through, the experiences that molded us and made us who we are. If you lie about your age, you diminish your own history.

There's nothing more exhausting than pretending to be younger than you are. So cut it out. The dress rehearsal is over – and it's:

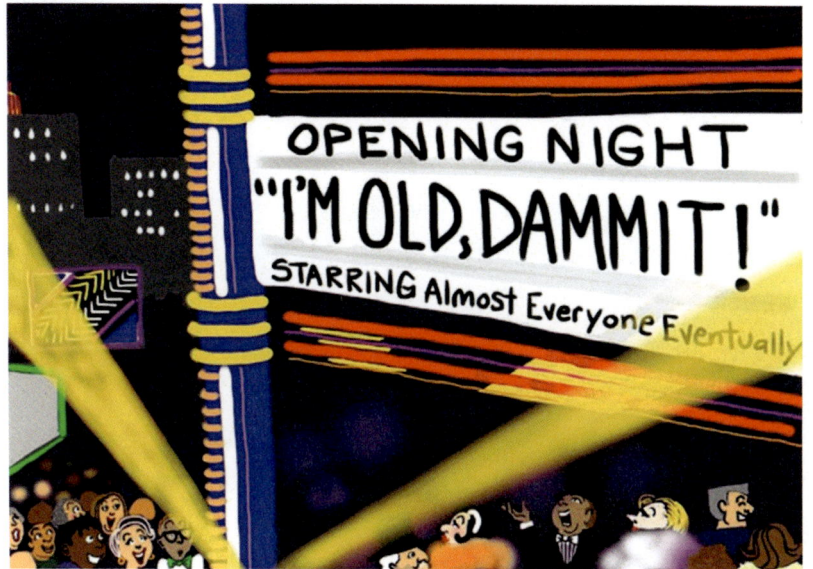

 ## number 4

Ignore advice on aging from Madison Avenue and New Age gurus since they'll make you lose your mind and your sense of humor. The older you get, the more you're going to need both.

You know what we're talking about.

To hear Madison Avenue beat its drums and crash its cymbals, you should be relentlessly stalking good looks, the ultimate tantric orgasm, nonstop optimism, the perfect perky, youthful wardrobe, and being the best YOU you can be well into your 90s.

In other words, successful aging Madison Avenue-style is like still being in high school – except with wrinkles.

Then, there's the latest beyond-the-Solar System declarations from one of those chipper, deluded New Age souls. They usually hang out in the produce section of your local Whole Foods, close to the organic red kale, and you will invariably see them on one of those days when you feel like a 17-car pileup, your jowls are sagging, and you haven't seen your libido in months.

Your ravaged appearance won't stop her, though. She'll take a cleansing breath and loudly announce:

(People with this kind of perky, annoying disposition always speak, write, and think with exclamation marks.)

Well. You might snarl that your 63-year-old body parts have not been notified of this good news. You might mention that you think 60 is the new 90 (or, on a particularly bad day, the new dead).

Or you might pretend to be so hard of hearing that you have to repeatedly ask your friend to repeat herself until she's screaming, so you can calmly reply:

Well, you don't have to shout!

Or you might simply smile enigmatically and say:

In fact, bullshit describes a lot of the advice you're bombarded with about aging. Try not to listen to it or step in it.

 number 5

Along the way, do remember how fortunate our generation of women has been.

OK, so you're not 24/7 ecstatic you're getting older. We get it. I mean, we really, really get it. We're there with you, sister.

But do remember a few things.

Unlike our mothers and their mothers, our generation of women grew up in an era of expanding choices and opportunities. We entered law, medical and graduate school in record numbers. We had careers and Ms. Magazine and feminism and Gloria Steinem. We had access to birth control – which changed everything. We no longer routinely died in childbirth, as women did for centuries. We could enter into contracts no matter what our marital status is and control our own money.

We grew up when it was a great time to be young — an exciting, confusing, crazy era of loud rebellion, more sexual freedom, deafening music, drugs, and grandiose dreams of changing the world.

Of course, we didn't change the world the way we wanted to. Wars still rage, inequality and poverty persist. But a quieter revolution in the lives of women has transformed American life and the workplace.

Look around. We may be our mothers' daughters.

But, we've been able to dream bigger and achieve more than they ever could. And as we age, we're healthier and more independent than they were. Most of us even still have our own teeth.

Which isn't to say you should be happy about your dwindling energy and the wrinkles and crepe-paper skin that have camped out on your body and don't seem to be moving on. Still, the barebones fact is, you either die or you grow old. And today, we're growing old at the best time in human history to be an aging woman.

No, it's not perfect. But the older and wiser you get, the more you figure out that perfection is almost never part of the equation, anyway.

 number 6

Appreciate your age for what it is: A different time in a long and varied life.

In his wonderful book, *Travels With Epicurus: A Journey to a Greek Island in Search of a Fulfilled Life*, Daniel Klein touts the advantages of being "authentically and contentedly old." He quotes Epicurus: "It is not the young man who should be considered fortunate, but the old man who has lived well, because the young man in his prime wanders much by chance, vacillating in his beliefs, while the old man has docked in the harbor, having safeguarded his true happiness."

Instead of constant striving and ticking off bucket lists, Klein suggests, we should appreciate this different time in our lives. With all our maintenance and exercise regimens and hair dye, we might look and feel pretty good. But we don't look young. We look like older women who look and feel pretty good.

And what's wrong with that?

 ## number 7

You're old enough to have a little perspective. Finally!

We'll give you a few examples:

You've lived long enough and lived through enough that you can redefine what "good fortune" really is.

We won't try to tell you that whatever doesn't kill you makes you stronger. Somebody – Nietzsche, evidently – already said it, and besides, people always line up to tell you that when you hit the inevitable hard times in your life.

What we will say is that the experiences of a longer life can make you more compassionate toward others and their misfortunes. And these life experiences can radically change your perspective on the world so that suddenly, if you're walking upright and not screaming with pain or hemorrhaging, you realize you're actually doing pretty well.

You can stop taking everything so damned personally.

The older you get, the closer you come to figuring out the world's a lot bigger than you are.

Like other byproducts of aging, this is a little disappointing – but somehow liberating.

You can also stop thinking you're special – and join the human race.

When you're young, you often need to think you are different, individual, special.

Something changes as you age, though. Maybe it's that your perspective has broadened and lengthened considerably. You begin to understand you're not as different or separate as you once thought. Instead, you realize we're all part of an immense continuum – following where our parents, grandparents and more distant ancestors have gone before us. We're also making way for those who follow us.

There's a poignance in leaving behind the idea we're special. But there's also a certain exhilaration in coming to understand we're part of something bigger than our own puny lives.

 number 8

You're too old to be vain.

Ha, ha, just joking about that! If you feel no vanity whatsoever, you should probably check yourself for a pulse.

You might be older, wiser, better and all that – but do you know anybody outside the graveyard who's completely devoid of vanity? Some things diminish, but never completely disappear.

Look at it this way: You may never be too old to be a little superficial. Maybe this is what people mean about being young at heart.

Just keep it in check. Wearing glasses, for example, may not make you look better, but they're a big improvement on the highly unattractive habit of blindly crashing into large pieces of furniture.

 **number 9**

You might be getting slower – but you're also getting smarter about what's really important.

Danish philosopher Soren Kierkegaard said that, "Life can only be understood backwards; but it is lived forward." Since Kierkegaard died when he was only 43, we can only assume that Scandinavians must acquire gravitas at a very early age.

The point is, you don't really comprehend the arc of a long life when you're young. You start out, as we all do, close to home. And, of course, you want to leave and rebel and travel as far and as fast as you can. You're fired by a fierce ambition and you want to be somebody.

Time passes – years and decades. You go far, you don't go as far as you want to, you succeed some, you fail some, you get the ever-loving crud knocked out of you, you get up, you fall down again, you realize success isn't as important as you once thought it was and it doesn't satisfy you for long, you begin to understand that failure might break your heart but it won't kill you – and that, even more important, you learn more from it than you do from success.

At some point – maybe in your late fifties or early sixties or later or maybe never – you may feel a greater sense of peace. You don't rage or want or aspire the way you used to. At this point in life, you are who you are.

You don't have much of anybody to impress. (Hell – a lot of them are dead, anyway.)

Friends – whose numbers have been diminished by illness or death – are more dear. Assuming you're still speaking to everybody in your family, you want them to be closer to you.

If you are fortunate enough to be healthy and loved and free from extreme hardship, you finally understand the joy of contentment. It's a word you probably didn't use when you were young, since it was so pallid and lackluster and quiet. But, at this point in life, it has a comforting warmth to it.

Contentment. When you were younger, would you ever have thought that might be more than enough?

 ## number 10

Sure, science is fickle. But it consistently shows older people are happier than younger people. *Happier!* Did you get that?

According to most psychological studies, people are happier as they age than they were in their 20s. They're also less neurotic and less depressed. If they're married, they're happier in their relationships than they've ever been.

Happier – when everybody assumes older people are miserable since they're so, well, *old*.

Why? Nobody knows. Maybe because you've finished the great responsibilities of life, such as picking a mate, rearing kids, and finding a career – and life's gotten simpler, with fewer responsibilities. Or because you've finally gotten more perspective and know you can deal with life's ups and downs and sheer craziness.

Maybe it's just because you've survived being young. Or maybe some of your nerve endings have died off and you're just not as overly sensitive or as pathologically neurotic as you used to be.

The fact is, happiness doesn't need a reason. It simply exists to be enjoyed – especially when it's unexpected.

 **number 11**

Some of us are better at being old than we were being young.

    While many of your friends your own age bewail the loss of youth, it might occur to you that you, for one, don't miss it that much.

    Some of us are better off now than we were when we were young. In fact, some of us are a hell of a lot freer and happier to be older than we were being young. This is known as the extremely late bloomer phenomenon. If you're one of these extremely late bloomer types, you're not over the hill – you're in your prime.

    Think of your bygone youth this way: Remember when you went through menopause? At first, it was a little upsetting. After all, you'd been fertile since you were an adolescent and it had defined your life in many ways. Even if you didn't want to get pregnant again, you were still being robbed of that possibility. Who were you if you weren't a fertile woman?

    But now? Do you really miss the PMS, the cramps, the pregnancy scares, the tampons? Think of your lost youth that way – kind of like an old tampon. When you see a tampon these days, you have to scratch your head to remember what you were supposed to do with it and why you even needed it in the first place.

Two: You're Entitled to an ATTITUDE

number 12

Come up with a great role model for unapologetic aging.

Face it. Everybody needs a role model now and then. The older you get, the older and more uncompromising your role models should be.

We're not talking about one of these plastic surgery miracles who's 90 but looks 35. We're talking about somebody who's accomplished, who's talented, who has presence. They're not young and they don't pretend to be.

Think Betty White or Maggie Smith, Hillary Clinton or Helen Mirren, Ray Wylie Hubbard or Willie Nelson. They're the kind of people who make you proud to be old.

Like all of them, you can be old in a cool and interesting way – or you can just be old. It's your choice.

 **number 13**

You might as well speak up.

Maybe you've lived your life not asking for what you want, since you might come across as a bitch. Well, cut it out. It's time to ask for what you want.

Anyway, at this point in your life, people won't think you're a bitch. They'll think you're an old bitch.

This is preferable to dying with your mouth hammered shut and having people refer to you as a saint at your funeral. The meek might inherit the earth, but it's not worth the wait.

number 14

Don't apologize to anybody for being a little older and slower.

Based on our own lives and rumors we hear, we can safely announce it's a scientific fact women apologize more than men. Maybe that's not a bad thing, since an eloquent apology has all the grace of a lovely haiku. Or maybe men should be apologizing more.

Whatever.

The point is, most women have already spent a good part of their early lives apologizing for something, for everything, for the failures of the whole damned world. Our natural inclination, as we age, is to now apologize for being older. And slower. And not being up with the latest trends.

You know what? Why don't we give it a rest? Do we really want to spend our golden years cringing and begging the world to pardon us for a long, boring list of imagined shortcomings?

Why don't we swear to ourselves that we will only apologize for crimes like homicide, rudeness, and tipping poorly? Why don't we work on a better, more dignified and defiant attitude about aging?

How hard can it be to be a little imperious? Haven't we earned the right? Or do naturally imperious women even ask themselves that question?

You know the answer to that: Hell, no.

 number 15

Celebrate every chance you get.

The older you get, the more funerals and memorial services you'll go to. But you've probably already noticed that.

Suddenly, you're dropping everything to hop a plane to go to a long-lost friend's service or hotfooting it across town to attend a neighbor's funeral. Those sad occasions always seem to motivate you into action. After all, they're the last chance you'll have to pay homage to someone who's meant something to you.

Why don't you try to give equal time to celebrating life's joyous occasions, though?

Make it a point to go to a far-flung friend's or family member's birthday or anniversary. Show up at a graduation or wedding. Throw a party for yourself or for someone else. Insist on taking part in something that's fun – even if you have to create an occasion. Break out the champagne. Spread the flowers everywhere. Crank up the music so that even your deafest friends can hear.

Life's growing even shorter and more precious as the years pass. So are your aging friends and loved ones. Seize every opportunity you can to get together and laugh. Don't wait for the sad times. Celebrate Wednesdays, if necessary. You can always rest on Thursday.

 number 16

Be grateful, dammit.

Robert Solomon, a University of Texas at Austin philosophy professor, scholar and writer, died suddenly and too young in 2007. But he left behind a large body of work, including this memorable quote:

"Gratitude, I want to suggest, is not only the best answer to the tragedies of life. It is the best approach to life itself."

At this time of life, all of us have losses – friends, family members, health, energy. The world as we knew it when we were young is changing – and sometimes it's easy to despair. Solomon's approach to life doesn't change what's happening, but it's a better way to live and experience the world.

Despair when you have to despair; some days, there's no choice. Life can be bleak and pitiless.

But that makes it even more important to remember how much you're grateful for.

Look back at the life you've lived and the people you have loved. Count your damned blessings. Sure, it's a cliché, and yeah, it's probably mawkish, too. So what?

Taking pleasure in the good and wringing every last bit of fun and humor from the world every chance you can is the only way to go through this life.

Three: Stay Flexible About the Whole Damned Thing

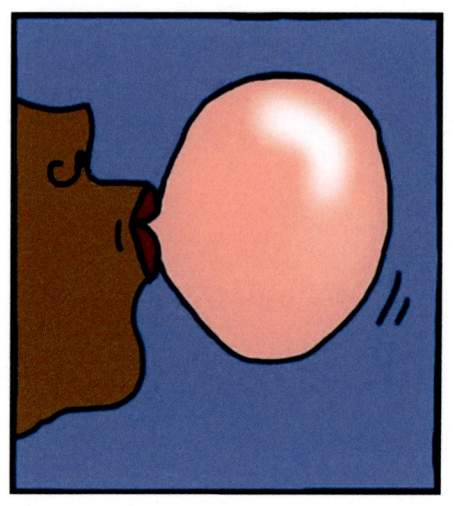

 ## number 17

For one thing, don't moan too much about being invisible. Not being seen has definite advantages.

You know the rumor: Women become invisible as they age. The world stops noticing us. Strange men don't propose marriage or more indecent acts or follow us in droves. Heads don't swivel, conversations don't stop and jaws don't drop as we pass by.

(Hell, for some of us, this never happened anyway, even when we were at our youngest, best and sexiest. But never mind! We're not bitter. As Nora Ephron memorably wrote, non-beautiful women don't lose their looks as they age; they may, in fact be *gaining* them.)

But, anyway – invisibility. Maybe it sucks, but it also has its advantages. People don't mess with you the way they used to. Since you look so mature and respectable and harmless — they never suspect you of anything scandalous or nefarious. You could take up shoplifting, cutting in line, drug-smuggling, shameless eavesdropping, or any other outrageous behavior at this age and probably get away with it. Not that you'd want to do anything like that. Certainly not! But it's a nice thought on a slow day.

 ## number 18

And yeah, the world lowers its expectations of you as you age. So why don't you take advantage of it?

You can see this as being insulting – or you can revel in the fact that, as long as you have your shoes on the right feet and appear to be standing upright, everyone thinks you're quite remarkable.

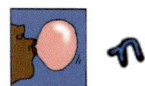 **number 19**

Even being hard of hearing has its upside.

As you and your friends and significant other age, you may reap benefits beyond Social Security and Medicare. Maybe your memory isn't as sharp as it used to be – but neither is theirs. Ditto for your hearing.

What this means is that you may end up having the same fascinating conversations over and over again without realizing it.

Or having a tete-a-tete like this:

You see! You thought you wouldn't have anything to talk about after the kids grew up and left home. Now, you realize, you may have decades of screaming:

at each other.

We call this marital communication at its finest.

number 20

Once you get over your initial childish resistance, you can go to movies and other events more cheaply.

The first time you ask for a senior discount at the movie theater can be extremely traumatic. You might delay it for weeks or months.

When you finally screw up the courage to identify yourself as a senior, you will probably hope that the person behind the counter will doubt your age and demand your driver's license since "you look awfully young to be a senior." (Word to the wise: This never happens. You hear us? Never. To the adolescent behind the cash register, we are all ancient. End of story.)

Once you've finally broken through the I Am a Senior shame spiral, though, you will find it remarkably easy to ask for it in the future. And not in a low voice, either.

After all, there are plenty of things to be legitimately embarrassed about in life – such as chewing with your mouth open, being rude to someone who's waiting on you, or running over a pedestrian.

Asking for a senior discount doesn't even rate as behavior to be embarrassed about. As long as you're polite about it.

 number 21

You can even kick the bucket list if you want to.

In recent years, somebody came up with the scintillating idea that our generation should have a bucket list. In other words, so that we wouldn't go gentle into that good night, we could, instead, sky dive, swim with the whales or dolphins or any other seafaring mammals, trek to Machu Picchu or ride a roller-coaster with our hands up.

Which is fine. You should empty your bucket list if that's what appeals to you.

But, remember: Not everybody wants to go screaming bloody murder into that good night.

At an age when you already have to undergo routine colonoscopies, bone-density exams, emergency hair-color appointments and the constant threat of blowing out your knees, you may realize you want to clear your life of petty obligations you never enjoyed, anyway. This is widely known as the fuckit list and may include such activities as monthly attendance at any boring book clubs, camping out, reading James Joyce, becoming a vegan, wearing stilettos, tasting liver, eliminating sugar, running a marathon, and getting anything but your floors waxed.

Isn't it a relief not to have to do things you never wanted to do, anyway? You're old enough to say no.

 number 22

You don't have to care as much as you used to about what everybody thinks.

 number 23

You can give toxic friends the heave-ho.

When we were younger, many of us steadfastly stayed "friends" with people who didn't really like us or wish us well – the sort of people who exhausted us emotionally. You know, the kind of pal who flayed us in public and private, prefacing her remarks with, "Don't take this the wrong way, but … " The alleged intimate who was clearly a little delighted with our misfortunes.

Remember?

When you're older, you finally reach the point when you realize how precious time is. If a "friend" is toxic and depletes you, what are you waiting for? Scream adios and show her the door.

After all, the world is full of wonderful people you can enjoy, people who will nourish you. Why settle for anything less? There's nothing more important to your quality of life than friends who truly care about you.

 number 24

You don't have to be as competitive as you used to be.

You may notice you're not as driven and competitive as you used to be when you were younger. For example, the news that an old rival has succeeded brilliantly might have once been devastating. Now, it's just a little annoying – if that.

Realizing that, *Oh, hell, we're all going to die anyway, so what difference does it make?* is sobering, of course.

But it's also so damned liberating.

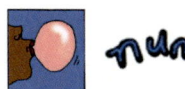 **number 25**

Sure, you can stretch your body and mind with yoga or pilates. But don't let anybody boss you around so much you end up hurting yourself instead of helping. It's *your* body and *your* mind, not the teacher's.

Yoga and pilates are great for older women, and many of the teachers are fine. Just avoid any teachers who are a little too messianic, overbearing, and try to push you when your body's screaming NO.

You're supposed to listen to your body in these disciplines, not tell it to shut up so you can satisfy somebody else's preening ego. Getting dragged out of a class by the paramedics is usually a pretty strong sign your body is saying it told you the teacher was an egotistical jerk.

# number 26

You don't have to give up your dreams as you age. But you may need to adjust them a little.

Let's be blunt.

No, you will probably not marry Paul McCartney.

And no, you will probably not become a famous Hollywood actress. (The latter disappointment occurs because the Hollywood formula seems to be that leading men should be roughly three decades older than their leading ladies. *How can you make it as an actress when all your potential leading men are already dead and pushy broads like Helen Mirren and Meryl Streep are hogging the best roles for women of a certain age?*)

New Year's resolutions, too, require the same sort of yoga-esque flexibility. Remember starting every year with a batch of resolutions centering on self-improvement? You were going to read great books, eat better, exercise more, go for your dreams, improve your posture, your attitude, your complexion. (Sure, it never happened. But you *thought* it might – once you recovered from your usual New Year's Eve hangover and everything.)

The years pass and you end up with different goals, such as not losing what you have any faster than you have to. Routine maintenance and emergency repairs don't have the same glamour as youthful anything-is-possible joie de vivre. But they do acquire a certain attractiveness when you consider the alternative.

The alternative is total surrender, obviously. What did you think we were talking about?

 number 27

You'll have to read between the lines – and go deeper – if you want to get any wisdom on aging from pop music.

One of the great inequities between older and younger birthdays hits you with all the subtlety of a mack truck when you turn 61 and realize lyricists are focused on younger years with songs such as "Sweet Little Sixteen." Nobody, you will notice (with just a soupcon of bitterness), seems to have penned any paeans to "Sweet Little 61."

In fact, one of the few songs we know of that focus on later years is the Beatles' "When I'm 64."

Remember when the song came out – how old and unreachable that age seemed then? And remember, too, that only two of the Beatles ended up living that long?

That kind of puts everything into perspective, when you think about it.

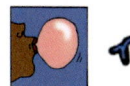 ## number 28

Aging men and women are treated differently. It really sucks. Dwell on this unfair fact of life as much as you have to, breathe deeply, then live your life, and go on.

You may not be familiar with the definition of "osmosis," which is described by Wikipedia as: "the net movement of solvent molecules through a partially permeable membrane into a region of higher solute concentration, in order to equalize the solute concentration on the two sides."

However, you are probably well-acquainted with some aging males' bright idea they can acquire youth by osmosis simply by marrying a far younger woman. Especially if you have a personal history with one of these men, you may have strong feelings that this kind of desperate maneuver is unfair, tasteless, sexist and ageist. In fact, you may have screamed these sentiments at the top of your lungs upon occasion.

After you've recovered your voice and your equilibrium, remind yourself that some ancient Romeos end up with squalling infants – which is the ultimate acquisition of youth by osmosis. This can be particularly satisfying to ponder as you are jetting off to Paris with your own new conquest and a good bottle of champagne. If Paris and the conquest don't materialize, a bubble bath and a good night's sleep can often improve your mood, as long as they are accompanied by enough champagne.

Still, you're right. It's unfair that men and women face different realities in the world as they age. It's unfair and it sucks and the whole world needs to change yesterday.

But here we are – in the middle of this imperfect world.

All we can do is handle our own lives as seriously and gracefully as possible, and love and support our friends as well as we can. Don't give the Straying Old Goats, vengeful notions, or bitterness any more room in your mind or heart than you have to. You have better things to do with your life.

Four: Mingle

 **number 29**

Take an interest in the young – whether they're related to you or not.

If you don't feel as if you were a perfect parent to your own kids, being a grandparent gives you a clean slate with a new generation. It's not a fulltime job and your responsibilities are only temporary. Even better, the bar is so much lower that being above-ground is considered a great asset.

And, if you're not a grandparent, remember you don't have to be a blood relation to make a difference in the life of a child. Why not try?

 number 30

Make friends of all ages. It's remarkable what you can learn from one another.

You're the sum total of all your decades of experience and wisdom, joys and hardships. You have a lot to offer the young.

And being around them can be great fun for you, too, especially if you manage to break them of the habit of constantly checking their smart phones. They're energetic, they're fresh, they have new ideas, they look at the world differently. It's enlightening and stimulating to be around them.

Also, do recall that younger friends:
1. can help you navigate your computer, TV and smartphone apps;
2. might be interested in your great store of knowledge about life (assuming they are not your own kids, of course);
3. could actually ask for your advice and listen to it;
4. can read the fine print;
5. and might be fascinated by your stories about the old days when people actually had to memorize phone numbers and remember friends' birthdates.

 number 31

And don't resent the young. They've got enough problems already.

Read the studies. The young aren't that happy. They're struggling with college loans, finding a job, looking for a mate, deciding whether to have kids. Remember how hard that was?

Sure, they look good — the same way we all did when we were young. But does anybody realize it at the time? Of course not. Nobody does. You finally figure it out decades later, when you're peering at old photos of yourself. "Why was I so critical of this photo?" you'll mutter, perplexed. "I looked so great! I looked so ... *young*."

That's the problem. Part of being young is a failure to appreciate how temporary youth is.

When you're young, you're also required to slavishly waste your hours by multi-tasking and telling everybody how busy and successful you are (and worrying that they're busier and more successful than you are). And sleeping off hangovers, weekend after weekend.

In fact, the young are so busy and driven, they can't even appreciate how delicious a long nap can be.

Also, do remember that today's young women are getting bikini waxes or having their pubic hair sculpted into hearts and other curlicues. These are procedures many of them describe as excruciating – and expensive.

If they only knew! As the years pass, nature gives us all a pretty good wax. It's painless and it's free.

 number 32

Also, don't automatically criticize the younger generation. It makes you sound like a bitter old bat.

You've probably noticed that some of your friends routinely trash the younger generation.

Well, you can certainly join in if you'd like. It's easy. And, after all, nothing puts roses in your cheeks like a little spirited criticism.

But wait. Sure, kids today can be thoughtless and self-absorbed and full of great and ridiculous dreams – but isn't that the hallmark of youth? Like us and every other preceding generation, they're only passing through.

Their clothes and slang and body decor may change, but they're still possessed by the same longings and great dreams and raging insecurities and delusions we had at the same age. Some things don't change at all.

Our parents criticized us, theirs criticized them, and so on, throughout history. To the older generation, the young are always hopeless and deplorable and doomed to failure.

Why join in that kind of kneejerk tirade against youth?

Do you want to be that predictable?

Really?

number 33

Before you complain that younger women aren't feminists, stop and look at the work of Tina Fey and Amy Poehler and Caitlin Moran and Lena Dunham. Those women kick some serious ass.

 number 34

Oh, and by the way, it's not your imagination and you're not paranoid. Baby Boomers really *are* that unpopular.

In his 1998 book, former NBC anchor Tom Brokaw decided our parents were members of *The Greatest Generation* since they went through the Great Depression and World War II and never complained about it.

Ever since then, it's been a terrifying plummet for the general reputation of Baby Boomers – whose Greatest Generation parents always said they'd never amount to anything, anyway, since they were spoiled, lazy, war-protesting hippies who smoked dope and lived in sin. (They may have been the Greatest Generation but they were really kind of judgmental.).

Maybe somebody will come forward and pen a book proclaiming Baby Boomers are even greater than their parents' generation, since we've given the universe great treasures like spandex, Spanx, blue jeans for dress-up occasions, recreational drugs, health food, Led Zeppelin, California wines and 24/7 news. .

If this doesn't happen – *fast*, we're going to have to comfort ourselves with the knowledge they're all going to miss us when we're gone. In the meantime, maybe we should just blackmail the rest of the world by threatening to have sex in public, the way we used to.

Jive: Dress and Undress

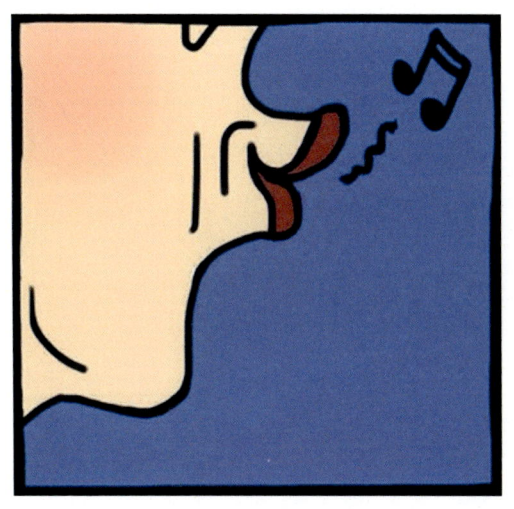

 number 35

Stilettos look great and sexy and all that. But remember that losing your balance in them, crashing into the punch bowl, and knocking out all your front teeth look a little less sexy and attractive – except to your dentist, maybe.

Some older women can still pull off the vertiginous heels, look stunning, and remain upright. More power to them.

Some of the rest of us, though, only aspire to fashionable flats and receive constant thank-you notes from our liberated feet and unbroken glass containers.

 **number 36**

Skinny jeans can look wonderful. Just make sure they're worth the effort.

Namely, you have to struggle to get in and out of them, you need to make sure you're not serving up a butt crack to the rest of the world (which is unattractive at any age, in our opinion, unless you've come to repair the toilet), and you don't mind spilling out over the low-rise cut.

Otherwise, they're fine. Unless you find you're more cheerful and alert when you're comfortable and can breathe easily. In that case, head for the spandex, which we happen to think is the greatest fashion discovery since the zipper.

 **number 37**

Wearing clothes intended for the very young can make you look ridiculous. But maybe you don't give a damn.

We say make yourself happy. Everybody else can go perform unnatural acts on themselves.

 **number 38**

Good, chic clothes are nice. We love them. But the attitude you wear is more important than anything else.

Look at the older women who pose for Ari Seth Cohen's lovely Advanced Style blog. Some are gorgeous, some aren't. Some are dressed beautifully, some are dressed eccentrically, some are dressed in ways you can't quite classify.

What unites all these women, though, are joie de vivre, fearlessness, and spirit. That kind of spark is more attractive and life-enhancing than any Chanel or Missoni.

 **number 39**

According to the research, you may find your sex drive increases after menopause. Or it may disappear. Or it may be the same. Got that?

Female sexuality, researchers note, is far more complicated and nuanced than male desire. We're glad they're finally paying attention, even if they haven't come up with any answers yet.

 number 40

If your sex drive needs a boost, the worst possible thing you can do is watch a Cialis ad on TV.

She hops up and down on one foot. She runs in the rain and laughs in a deranged manner. She dances to the music on her headphones and shakes her finger to the rhythm, with a disturbed grin on her face.

That's what he's always loved about her – that she's too stupid to find her other shoe or use an umbrella or spare the rest of the world the sight of her tragically spasmodic dance moves. The syrupy music swells and so does something else, since he's been popping Viagra like M&Ms and it's impossible to find good, sleazy pornography these days when there's a warrant out for your arrest.

Or, no! Wait! Maybe they're taking out the trash together or raking leaves together. He looks up and she looks up and their eyes meet, the way one's eyes always meet when one is taking out the trash or raking the leaves or one is cross-eyed. Everything swells and pretty soon they're in separate bathtubs, the meaning of which is apparent to no one.

So this is what happened to the Baby Boomer generation, which practically invented sex and did it in the road and in the car and at Woodstock, aided and abetted by loud rock music and handfuls of illegal drugs. But now the drugs are prescription and the music is sappy and erotic as a mouthwash jingle, and our formerly overheated and oversexed generation is being reduced to being encouraged to hump over clean laundry or raked leaves while drippy music tinkles like a leaky bladder.

Who cares what Cialis does or doesn't do? Its ads are enough to turn anybody permanently off sex and force them to join the nearest celibate religious order, where there is no such thing as cable TV. Avoid them – or lose your remaining shreds of libido.

 number 41

This can be an especially good time of life for sex, whether you're with another person or a device.

Think about it. You no longer have to worry about getting pregnant or catching an STD or developing a reputation as an elderly slut. You don't have anything to prove. All you have to do is let go and enjoy yourself.

Orgasms may take a little longer. But, as one researcher noted, people who have orgasms seem a little happier; they walk around with goofy grins on their faces. At this age, anything that gives you a goofy grin is worth a little more time.

 number 42

If, on the other hand, your sex drive has waned some, think of all the leftover time and energy you can now devote to pursuits like world peace and a cure for rudeness.

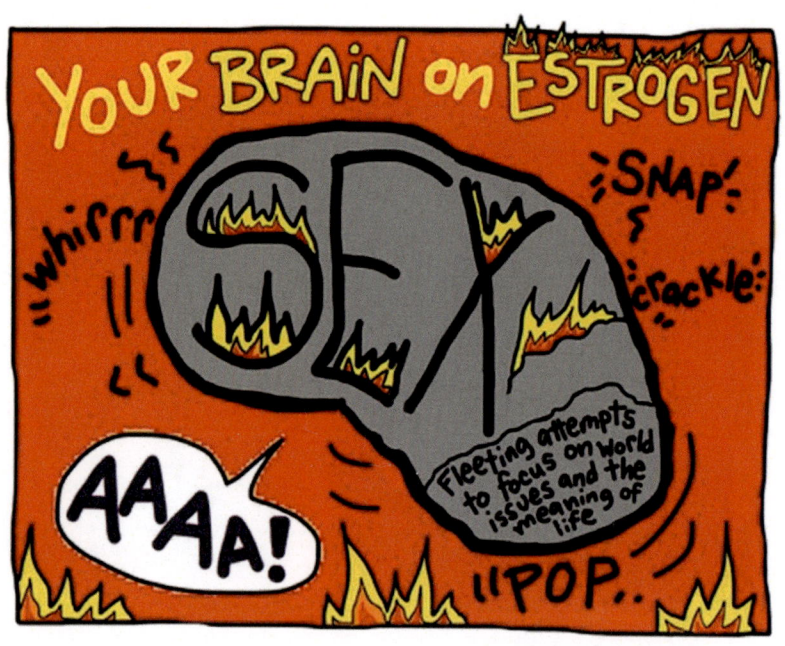

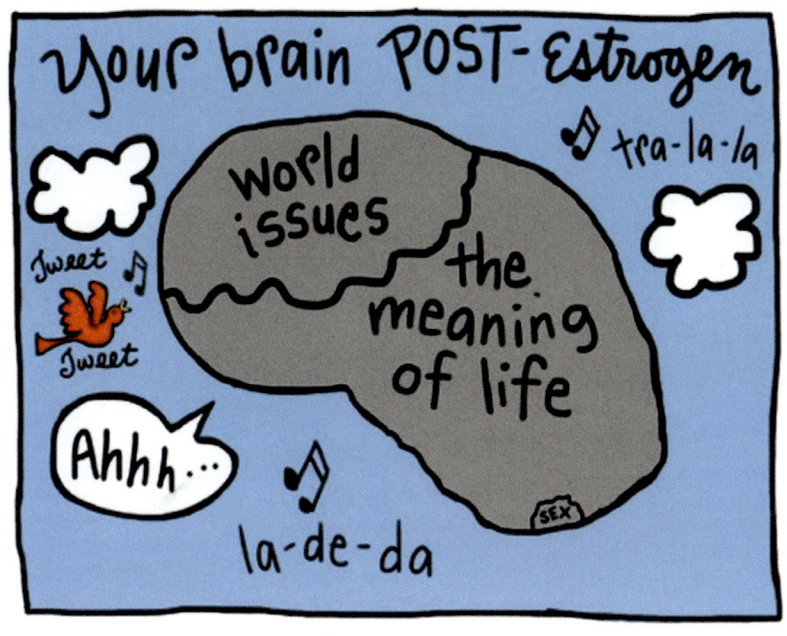

Six: Grab a Quick Fix if Necessary

 **number 43**

Whenever possible, hire someone to help you do small jobs you can't or don't want to do.

And forget feeling guilty about it. You're stimulating the economy.

number 44

Sometimes you need to go whole hog and throw yourself a pity party.

Oh, sure. Self-pity gets a bad rap. "I'm not throwing a pity party for myself," you'll hear someone announce from time to time. That kind of negative attitude is quite predictable in a country settled by tough and joyless Puritans.

But hold on. There is a time and place for everything – even Puritanism (17th-century New England, to be precise).

Similarly, self-pity. It may be called for and indulged in when the skies have opened up and rained excrement on you, when you're sick of trying to be cheerful and you only want to cry or scream, when a friend has died or gotten a bad diagnosis, when you're low, when you feel washed up, when the wrong putz won the election, when you feel like shit, when every square inch of your body and skin aches.

At times like this, you should remember there are perfectly good reasons why bubble baths, Jeni's Salty Caramel ice cream, wine, trashy magazines, and other legal indulgences were invented.

Sure, you might not want to make a constant habit of it – but tonight, why don't you throw the grandmother of all pity parties? Keep the invitation list brief, and no one but you will ever know.

number 45

When you're getting patronized a little too much in a restaurant, you can "accidentally" turn over the flower vase. Unless you want to be more subtle.

We're talking about the ubiquitous, uber-friendly young waiter or waitress who thinks it's cute to call you "young lady."

As with many minor conundrums in life, you can handle this in a variety of ways that don't involve breaking glasses or china:

1. Take the high road and ignore it, reassuring yourself that eventually somebody else will snap the kid's head off;
2. Quietly point out to the server that, although well-intentioned, this kind of joking reference is clumsy and insulting;
3. Announce that young ladies, real or pretend, rarely tip well. Older women treated with deference and slavish respect, however, have been known to lavishly reward their servers.

If none of these approaches works, however, you may have to embrace your status as a thin-skinned grump — and tell your server to stick it where the sun don't shine.

 ## number 46

Just because the rest of the world is on an automatic first-name basis doesn't mean you have to join in. No, ma'am.

We live in an informal, chummy world. Our banks want to have "relationships" with us. Our co-workers say we're family. Receptionists and business phone callers and other total strangers want to call us by our first names so we can all be equal – even though they're 40 years younger than you are and you couldn't pick them out of a police lineup.

All of which may strike you as sweetly naïve. Or purely annoying. Or borderline stalker-ish.

If you are feeling disgruntled, you might reply to your would-be intimate: "I'm sorry, but only my close friends call me by my first name." Either that, or find yourself a nametag that identifies you as the Duchess of Windsor.

 number 47

You are as tall as you were the last time you agreed to be measured.

After years of being a certain height, you may notice you're not quite as towering as you used to be. Either the world's getting bigger or you're getting smaller.

If you don't want to torture yourself with reports of your own shrinkage, simply refuse to get measured the next time you're in the doctor's office. Tell the nurse you've always been 5'7 and you see no reason to be re-measured. Look her or him straight in the eye and don't budge.

If this doesn't work, a casual remark about your tendency to lose control of your bladder when you're upset should suffice.

number 48

When you're having a rotten day, you might as well entertain yourself with a few harmless dreams.

For example:
1. You know how your laptop, tablet and cellphone bombard you with constant notices for upgrades? Well, why can't your wayward body do the same thing?

    Imagine hitting a button to upgrade your back, your feet, your teeth. More notices to come tomorrow, in case any other body part needs improvement. We're betting on your knees.
2. As long as we're pursuing impossible dreams, let's rip the word "spry" from our national vocabulary. After that, we'll take on "feisty."
3. Most of us live in terror of developing Alzheimer's or some other dementia. Misplace your car keys and you don't feel like a madcap heiress, you feel like you're 15 seconds away from entirely losing your mind.

    Scientific research on dementia is promising if you happen to be in kindergarten right now. If you're older than that, its slowness makes you twitchy and apoplectic.

    The 21st century might be a decent time to be an aging woman, but it's not a perfect time. A perfect time would include an immediate cure for dementia, as well as the option to erase certain untoward memories, such as 1970s fashions, 1980s hair, disastrous affairs, and all of Rod McKuen's poetry. Let's all dream about that one, as long as we're at it.

 number 49

When you complain, make it artful.

Look at it this way: At every age, you have to make decisions.

When you're younger, you have big choices about going to college, taking illicit drugs, having constant sex, getting married, having kids, buying a house, staying married, making money – you know, all those really tough choices you're glad are behind you, even if some of them felt pretty damned good at the time.

Anyway — if you can get your mind out of the sex, drugs and rock'n'roll gutter — now that you're older, you still have all kinds of big decisions to make. We're talking about complaining, of course.

You know how it is. We all have days when our feet hurt, our stomach's a little sour, our tooth implant's taking eons and costing a fortune. That kind of lousy day. When somebody asks how you are, you're dying to unload every stinking detail about how aging sucks and your body's falling apart AND HOW YOU WISH YOU'D GOTTEN DENTURES INSTEAD OF THAT MISERABLE TOOTH IMPLANT AND –

Well! That kind of tirade can clear a room pretty quickly. Just try it if you don't believe us.

Face it: Who wants to be known as the grouchy old witch if you don't have to? You really do have a choice here. You can curdle your soul with bitterness and a litany of what's gone wrong. Or you can suck it up and:

— *Say you're doing swell. Then ask about the other person.* This is how generations of Southern women have been taught to respond to adversity. Of course, it has certain drawbacks (e.g., ulcers, clenched teeth, a tendency toward feelings of martyrdom, and the distinct possibility of morphing into the hysterical excesses of the aging woman in a Tennessee Williams play). Still, it lends a certain smoothness to superficial social situations in which no one truly wants to know the horrific details of your life no matter how old or young you are.

— *Learn to complain in an amusing way.* Yes, complaining can be an art form. We, personally, have worked at it for years – in newspaper columns, cartoons, blog posts, magazine articles, you name it. In fact, our view is that if it's funny enough, it doesn't even count as complaining. Witness, for example, Washington, D.C. doyenne Alice Roosevelt Longworth. After a cancer diagnosis and bilateral mastectomy, she widely referred to herself as "the only topless octogenarian in Washington." If your health-related remarks are this amusing, they shouldn't even count as complaints. In fact, you can dine out on them for years.

— *Tie your complaints into some larger philosophical context that give the impression you aren't completely self-absorbed, but are painfully aware of the hopelessness of the human condition.* So, after, say, several minutes of your own complaints (we all get carried away, sometimes), lean back, smile gently and say, "Oh, but what was it that Oscar Wilde said? Oh, yes! 'We are all in the gutter, but some of us are looking at the stars.' "

Then retreat quickly in order to leave the impression you are one of the star-gazers.

 number 50

Be realistic – and remember that not everything can be fixed quickly now or ever.

Nothing will ever completely make up for the losses of friends or good health as you age. All you can do is to continue to engage with the world, try not to lose your curiosity about life, and drink heavily, when necessary.

 number 51

Unfortunately, one thing that works best is not a quick fix. Hint: It also involves sweating.

Every time you turn around, some new expert or another is exhorting you about the latest miracle antidote to aging, from vitamins to denial, red wine to Jesus. These miracle cures come, they go, they'll be back again. Hell, they'll probably outlive all of us.

There's only one approach everyone seems to agree on and nobody takes back: You have to keep moving if you want to be healthier. (Midnight trips to the refrigerator, evidently, do not count.)

So, save your vitamin money and invest in a new pair of exercise shoes. Use them day after day and replace as needed. It's not glamorous and it's not easy, but neither is life.

Seven: Be Prepared

 number 52

Considering surgical intervention? Just remind yourself of what happened to Olivia Goldsmith – and plan accordingly.

Go under the knife for plastic surgery? It's up to you – depending on your financial resources, how you look aging naturally, and how much you care about what you look like. Your chosen profession is also of great importance. (Writers and artists, fortunately, can afford to look more haggard than, say, models or actresses. In fact, the worse an artist or writer looks, the more depth and genius may be attributed to her. Or not. Anyway, it's a thought we like.)

We really aren't judgmental about plastic surgery, except for bad facelifts, which shouldn't happen to a French poodle.

But do remember that there are occasional fatalities during plastic surgery. Remember Olivia Goldsmith, who wrote the wonderful get-even novel, *The First Wives' Club*? She died during a chin lift.

Based on this cautionary tale, you should make specific plans if you choose to go forward with plastic surgery. Make sure 1) you have a top-flight surgeon and 2) leave behind an alternative excuse for your cause of death, such as a camping trip with disabled children or a pilgrimage to India to emulate Mother Teresa.

You know, just in case. You want people sobbing and wailing at your memorial service, not snickering at your fatal case of vanity and sneaking a look at your new chin.

 **number 53**

You're old enough to know how to react to others' bad news.

When something bad happens to a friend, some people struggle with what their response should be. They blurt out bromides like, "Well, time heals everything," or greeting-card philosophies such as, "You know, everything happens for a reason."

Worse, they may suggest someone bears responsibility for his or her own bad news. ("I *told* him to quit smoking" or "She should have been wearing a helmet if she wanted to ride a motorcycle. Which she shouldn't have been doing anyway.")

This kind of well-meaning, but blithering ineptness helps no one and may, in fact, lead to a glass of merlot being flung in the would-be comforter's face.

Life can be brutal and random, raining on the just, the unjust, and the vegan triathlete. You should be old enough and wise enough to realize tragedy and illness can be senseless and unfair.

When a friend is in pain, it's enough to say, "I'm so sorry." Just that and not much more. "I'm so sorry you're going through this."

 number 54

Even though we hate the word "pro-active," you should probably be pro-active about the defining facts of your life.

Let's put it this way: At a certain point in life, a smart woman shouldn't go anywhere without leaving behind a clearly marked folder of facts pertinent to her obituary.

Otherwise, she might find herself not only dead but posthumously mortified by an inaccurate birthdate, astrological sign, marital history, educational background, political affiliation or favorite charity.

 number 55

Keep your verbal talents honed.

When you were younger, you needed to know how to write a great term paper and deliver a funny, yet poignant toast at your best friend's rehearsal dinner.

As you age, you should know how to write a great obituary and deliver a funny, yet poignant eulogy.

Isn't it nice to know the required talents are roughly the same – even if the events are different?

 number 56

Trust us. Knowing what *not* to say in a eulogy is as important as knowing what to say.

Here is a true story. A wonderful woman and close friend died a few years ago. At her memorial service, guests were invited to come to the podium and speak about her. This kind of openness is certainly a lovely idea in theory.

Unfortunately, one of the people drawn to express his opinion that day began his comments with an enigmatic remark. "When I think of Mrs. R," he said, "I always think of the c-word."

This might have been fine had he immediately clarified which c-word, precisely, he was thinking about. But he didn't. He launched into a series of stories about Mrs. R, grinning fondly at all the memories. He talked and he talked and he talked, as the audience grew a bit restless and distressed, clearly wondering: *Can you tell us what the c-word is, so we can quit thinking about it?*

The young man was in no hurry, though. A good – or bad – 10 minutes later, he remembered his initial point – oh, yes! The c-word!

"It's for caring," he told the highly relieved crowd. "Mrs. R was very caring." Then he sauntered back to his seat.

There are many important lessons to be learned here: 1) memorial service free-for-alls are charming, but fraught with peril; 2) unless you're a professional speaker, impromptu talks at someone else's funeral should never be truly impromptu; and 3) just to be safe, don't let your audience's minds range too freely when it comes to c-words. Or any other letter that might begin an objectionable word.

If that cleans out the whole alphabet, then so be it.

 number 57

Sometimes you have to gird your loins to get your way. Whatever that means.

You can tell a lot about somebody's life from her memorial service.

Take this verse from Proverbs, which usually gets hauled out at services for women who have sacrificed their lives for their families: "Who can find a virtuous woman? For her price is far above rubies." Then it goes on to list how the virtuous woman works with wool and flax and plants vineyards and girds her loins and clutches the distaff and "eateth not the bread of idleness."

You can usually lay money on it: When the old price-of-rubies quote gets dusted off and everybody sobs about what an unappreciated doormat Old Mom was, they're probably just upset that now they're going to have to learn to do their own laundry.

You may have to gird your loins and clutch your distaff and get really explicit about it. Anybody who hauls out the Proverbs quote at your service will get haunted till the end of time.

 number 58

Make sure your last words aren't something tacky or incoherent gurgles.

Who knows whether Oscar Wilde's last words were really, "Either that wallpaper goes or I do"?

Or whether the departing thespian really said, "Dying is easy, comedy is hard"?

Or if the dying Gertrude Stein – when nobody could tell her what the answer was – then demanded, "In that case, what is the question?"

The point is, they all got credit for saying something memorable and witty before they expired. This has a certain appeal. If you have to die anyway – and the evidence seems a bit compelling – why not depart with a little verbal panache?

Fine, but: What if your last utterances turn out to be inarticulate gurgles? Or you're crossing a busy city street and get sideswiped by some hot-rodding creep in a pickup truck, and your last words are, "Screw you, you moron!" (The latter is understandable, but lacks a certain je ne sais quoi.)

You're going to have to think of choosing your last words as something similar to a prepaid funeral option – short on glamour, but long on thoughtfulness.

First, you'll need an accomplice. Pick somebody who 1) presumably won't predecease you; 2) has a good chance of showing up when you're in extremis; 3) shows up favorably in your will; and 4) isn't so literal-minded and unimaginative as to object to creative shading of the truth – *since, after all, this is going to be the last thing you ever ask him or her to do, dammit.* (If threats are necessary, so be it. We're talking about your reputation for eternity.)

 **number 59**

Whoever it was who said you should be prepared for anything never contemplated the possibility of adult diapers.

On the other hand, the proper attitude about adult diapers can enhance your reputation as an outrageous old broad who doesn't give a damn.

Eight: Be Someone Better

 number 60

Go deeper, not shallower.

Remember the defiant fashion models who stared into the TV camera and announced their intention to "fight old age" every step of the way?

Just an observation: Wouldn't they have been better off pouring their energy into securing world peace or a cure for cancer or an end to poverty? (Picture: "She Fought Old Age!" on your tombstone. Is that what you want?)

After all, if you're going to be getting older, anyway, wouldn't you like to be getting wiser and deeper?

 number 61

Our generation has the chance to make a big difference by aging well.

On a day when you're feeling fed up with the whole aging business, you should check out Laura Carstensen's book, *A Long Bright Future: Happiness, Health, and Financial Security in an Age of Increased Longevity*. Carstensen is the founding director of the Stanford Center on Longevity, a psychologist, and a remarkably tough-minded optimist who can make you look at aging in a new light.

Carstensen reminds us that our generation's sheer size and newfound longevity give us an unprecedented advantage and a responsibility to future generations. We can change society's ideas about aging by staying involved and productive and by making conscious choices about how we want to live these bonus decades of our lives.

We will still get old. But we have the opportunity to redefine how the world looks at aging — since we're Baby Boomers and are incapable of doing anything quietly or inconspicuously.

So, think about it. What kind of older woman do you want to be? Are you going to define yourself – or let other people define you? What do you want to learn? Where do you want to travel? What can you do to make the world a little better?

 **number 62**

Give other people a second chance. Like you, they may have improved with age.

If you've never enjoyed going to high school and college reunions, you might try them as you get older. There's a certain esprit de corps for having survived so long and for having lived through a number of train wrecks that life slams you with.

Look around. The older you all get, the more humility and the less hubris you see. Those people you never liked 40 or 50 years ago are different human beings now. And so, probably, are you.

 number 63

Be kind every chance you can get.

Have you heard the quote about being kind to everyone you meet, since they are all fighting great battles? Evidently, Plato said it.

Maybe it doesn't have anything specific to do with getting older, but it's something to think about. Around us and within us, great battles are going on. Once you realize that, you look at the world differently. Be kind to the battle-weary – which is all of us.

 **number 64**

How we deal with our sorrows and losses will define our lives.

If you're a parent, you may have realized that, the older your kids got, one of the greatest lessons you can teach them is about failure.

After all, failure shows up as reliably as the common cold in everyone's life. It arrives without fanfare and crushes your spirit into fine particles and temporarily saps your will to live or eat ice cream.

But then what? What do you do after you crawl out of fetal position and open your eyes? How do you recover from failure and go on? After you've cried and howled and bankrupted your cache of foul language – what you do then will determine the rest of your life. You do have choices, even if they're not the choices you wanted.

This time of life – our later years — is similar in many ways. We are all dealing with limitations and losses. Our knees are going, our feet hurt, our eyes are growing cataracts, and our minds sprouting barnacles. Oh, and people we care about are infirm or dying. It sucks.

But how are we going to handle it all? How are we going to move on and live as well as we can? When time is dwindling, it's even more important to use it well.

 number 65

You aren't just aging for yourself. You're aging for friends who didn't live long enough to grow old.

Every one of us who is aging has friends who didn't make it this far. They didn't survive to grow old – and we did. There's no fairness to any of this – just plain dumb luck.

They never had the chance to grow old, never got to complain about their wrinkles or wattles or jowls. They never made it to this time of life when, oddly, many of us feel happier than we've ever been before.

So, think about them and try to remind yourself that aging is a privilege. It's a privilege that carries heartaches and fears and pain – but still, it's privilege.

We are all aging for a host of people who haven't been as fortunate as we've been. It's up to us to do it well for ourselves and for our lost friends. What do you say we don't fuck it up?

THE AUTHORS

Ruth Pennebaker is the author of *Women on the Verge of a Nervous Breakthrough*, as well as three acclaimed young-adult novels, *Don't Think Twice*, *Conditions of Love*, and *Both Sides Now*. She also writes the popular blog, The Fabulous Geezersisters (geezersisters.com).

Ms. Pennebaker has been a columnist for the *Dallas Morning News* and the *Texas Observer*, and a commentator for Austin's public radio station KUT 90.5. Her work has appeared frequently in *The New York Times* and other nationwide publications. She lives in Austin with her mad-scientist husband, and they both seem to be aging pretty well. So far, anyway.

Marian Henley, a syndicated cartoonist from 1981-2002, wrote and illustrated the graphic novel, *Maxine*, the comic strip collection, *Laughing Gas*, and the graphic memoir, *The Shiniest Jewel*.

Ms. Henley's cartoons have been published widely in American newspapers and magazines such as *San Francisco Chronicle*, *Ms*, and *MAD*, as well as in publications in Italy, Spain, Russia, and Sweden. Her cartoon characters have appeared in video format on PBS, the Learning Channel, and in national television advertisements. She lives in Austin with her husband and son, plus multiple cats and dogs.

Book design by Mark D'Antoni, eBook DesignWorks

Copyright © 2014 by Ruth Pennebaker and Marian Henley

All rights reserved. No part of this publication may be reproduced, distributed, or transmitted in any form or by any means, including photocopying, recording, or other electronic or mechanical methods, without the prior written permission of the publisher, except in the case of brief quotations embodied in critical reviews and certain other noncommercial uses permitted by copyright law. For permission requests, please contact the authors at ruthpennebaker@gmail.com

ISBN 978-0-9862307-0-7

Made in the USA
San Bernardino, CA
07 November 2017